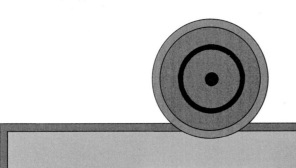

THE SUN

ROBERT DAILY

THE SUN

A FIRST BOOK
FRANKLIN WATTS
NEW YORK / CHICAGO / LONDON / TORONTO / SYDNEY

For JKD with love

Cover photograph copyright ©: NASA/JPL

Photographs copyright ©: National Optical Astronomy
Observatories/National Solar Observatory, Sacramento Peak: pp.
8, 23, 33, 39, 45; NASA/JPL: pp. 11, 24, 30, 35, 37, 40, 43, 53; The
Bettmann Archive: p. 14; Comstock/Georg Gerster: pp. 17, 48;
North Wind Picture Archive, Alfred, Me.: pp. 18, 21 right; Stock
Montage, Chicago: p. 21 left; Astronomical Society of the Pacific:
p. 28.

Library of Congress Cataloging-in-Publication Data

Daily, Robert.
   The sun / by Robert Daily.
      p.   cm. — (A First book)
   Includes bibliographical references and index
   ISBN 0-531-20105-8
      1. Sun—Juvenile literature. [1. Sun.] I. Title. II. Series.
QB521.5.D35 1994
523.7—dc20   94-2241   CIP   AC

CONTENTS

OUR STAR OF STARS

CHAPTER ONE

Once upon a time, there was (or *is*) a *star*. An ordinary, everyday, run-of-the-mill star.

This star is neither young nor old. It is only average in brightness; in fact, another star called Polaris (the North Star) shines about six thousand times brighter. (Most of the stars in the night sky shine brighter but are very far away from Earth.) It is only medium in size; in fact, some stars are hundreds or even thousands of times larger. And as for temperature, it is merely normal; some stars burn thousands of degrees hotter.

This particular star is located in the outer third of a cloud of stars called the Milky Way galaxy—though you might have a hard time

Our sun may look like just a normal, everyday star — but we couldn't live without it!

finding it there. There are between 100 billion and 250 billion other stars in the Milky Way! Not to mention the millions, maybe billions of *other* galaxies in the universe. In other words, locating this star is like trying to find a single grain of sand on a beach.

A humble, ordinary, hard-to-find star. So why do we care about it? Simple: It's our sun.

Yes, the sun—located at the center of our *solar system*—is a star like any other. But there is one difference. Although we can see many stars at night, the sun is the only star we can see during the day.

The sun may be average—but to us on Earth, it is a thing of wonder. Compared to other objects in our solar system, it is enormous! If the sun were hollow, it could hold a million Earths. It is ten times wider than Jupiter, the biggest planet. In terms of *mass*, the sun is 740 times more massive than the nine planets combined. It contains 99.9 percent of all the matter in our solar system.

The sun is not just the biggest object in the solar system; it is also the most important. Without the sun's powerful *gravity*, for example, all the planets would go flying off into space.

For life on Earth, the sun is especially important. It gives us food, wind, weather, and tides. It powers our factories and runs our automobiles—fuels such as coal and gas are nothing more than stored-up sunlight. Best of all, the sun produces light and heat. Without that light (or fuel created by that light), you wouldn't be reading this book. Without that heat, our planet would turn into a giant snowball. All life on Earth would be wiped out.

Yes, the sun is a very powerful thing. And this is why we begin our book with an important warning: NEVER, EVER LOOK AT THE SUN DIRECTLY, with or without a telescope! Doing this could damage your eyes or even blind you.

SUN FACTS

Our sun is known as a *yellow dwarf* because, compared to other stars, it is relatively small and yellow in color. (It only seems big and bright to us because we're so close, relatively speaking.) As we noted, some stars are many times bigger. But the majority of stars are smaller than our sun.

Looking at photos of the sun, we might think that it's a solid object like Earth. It definitely

The sun's gravity keeps the nine planets of our solar system from spinning into space. Seen in this composite photo are Earth (bottom right), Venus (bottom left), and (top left to right) Jupiter, Mercury, Mars, and Saturn. Earth's moon is in the foreground.

seems to have a solid surface. In fact, though, the sun is a fiery ball of gas, mostly made up of hydrogen (between 75 and 90 percent) and helium (between 10 and 25 percent). The word helium comes from the Greek word *helios*, meaning "sun." Carbon, nitrogen, oxygen, and tiny amounts of other elements make up the rest.

The sun is located at the center of our solar system, with the nine planets orbiting around it. The sun, however, is not just standing still. It has two motions: it spins on its *axis* (like Earth), and it journeys through the galaxy, dragging the solar system with it. It makes this longer trip at a speed of about 12 miles (20 km) per second.

Here on Earth we count on gravity, a strong but invisible force, to keep objects—as small as a baseball or as large as the moon—from drifting off into space. The sun's gravity is strong enough to keep all the planets (even Pluto, several billion miles away) in its *orbit*. The sun's gravity is twenty-eight times as strong as the pull at Earth's surface. If you weigh 100 pounds (45 kg) on Earth, you'd weigh more than 5,500 pounds (2,497 kg) on the sun!

STUDYING THE SUN

CHAPTER TWO

Ancient peoples knew they couldn't live without the sun, though they didn't know why. And so, almost from the beginning of recorded time, this fiery orb has been worshiped as a god.

The sun god was called Ra by the Egyptians, Helios by the Greeks, Marduk by the Babylonians, and Utu by the Sumerians. To the Aztecs, it was a bloodthirsty god named Huitzilopochtli, who they fed with human sacrifices. The Incas of South America believed their king was a descendant of the sun; their culture was based on sun worship.

The sun's motions inspired some interesting stories. The ancient Chinese, for example,

Ancient peoples worshiped the sun as a god.
This relief of Ra, the Egyptian god of the sun,
was found on a temple wall.

believed that the sun was chased across the sky by a giant dragon. When the sun temporarily disappeared because it was covered by the moon—an eclipse—they were afraid the dragon had swallowed the sun and was going to eat it. So they banged gongs, lit firecrackers, and shot arrows into the sky to drive away this evil spirit.

The Egyptians also worried when they couldn't see the sun. When it sank below the horizon every night, they thought it had to travel through an underground cave, fighting off demons before it could return the next morning.

Those same Egyptians (who built a civilization that lasted more than three thousand years) prayed to many different sun gods. There were gods of the rising and setting sun; of the sun's heat and the sun's light; of the sun's disk and the sun's rays. The Egyptians built their pyramids at Giza so the sides would be in a line with the rising sun at the vernal equinox (the beginning of spring).

Other ancient cultures designed structures to follow the sun's motions. Many scientists think the famous circle of stones at Stonehenge, in England, was built so the sun would rise over one of the big rocks when the sun appears to reach its highest point in the sky (the summer solstice). The Big Horn Medicine Wheel in Wyoming served a similar function for American Indians.

THE DAWN OF ASTRONOMY

Eventually people wanted not just to worship the sun, but to study and understand it.

The ancient Greeks were among the first to ask serious questions about the sun. Though they weren't always correct, they came up with some interesting theories. In the sixth century B.C., Anaximander of Miletus wrote that the sun "is like a chariot wheel, the rim of which is hollow and full of fire."

Also in the sixth century B.C., followers of the Greek mathematician Pythagoras concluded that Earth rotated around a "central fire" every twenty-four hours. Unfortunately, in the fourth century B.C., a fellow named Aristotle decided Earth was at the center of our universe, and not the sun. Twenty centuries would pass before the truth was widely accepted.

American Indians in Wyoming built this Big Horn Medicine Wheel so that the sun would rise over a certain rock at the summer solstice.

Early *astronomers* were concerned with basic questions about the sun—such as its size and distance from Earth. In the sixth century B.C., Heraclitus of Ephesus stated that the sun could be no bigger than 12 inches (30.5 cm) in diameter. One century later, his countryman Anaxagoras decided that the sun was "a mass of red-hot metal"—in other words, a burning rock—about 35

Pythagoras believed that Earth spun around a "central fire" like the sun. Unfortunately, more than twenty centuries passed before everybody agreed with his theory.

miles (56 km) in diameter. He also believed the sun was about 4,000 miles (6,400 km) away from Earth.

In the third century B.C., Aristarchus of Samos concluded that the sun was 720,000 miles (1,152,000 km) from Earth. He got this number by figuring the angles formed by the sun, Earth, and the moon. (Using the same method, he came very close to judging the distance between Earth and the moon.) In the next century, Hipparchus—known as the father of modern astronomy—decided that the sun was 5 million miles (8 million km) away and about seven times as large as Earth.

The Greek astronomers got closer and closer to the truth. But it wasn't until the twentieth century that we knew the sun's measurements: about 865,000 miles (1,392,082 km) in diameter, and an average of 92,975,700 miles (148,761,120 km) from Earth.

SCOPING THE SUN

After Hipparchus, it was a long time before scientists added anything new to the findings of the Greeks. Finally, in the sixteenth century, a Polish mathematician named Nicolaus Copernicus stated that the sun was indeed at the center of our universe. (The term *solar system* comes from the

Latin word *sol*, meaning "sun.") His book, *On the Revolutions of the Celestial Spheres*, came out on the day he died in 1543.

The telescope was invented at the beginning of the seventeenth century, and the Italian astronomer Galileo Galilei used it to prove that Copernicus was right—that the sun was at the center of the solar system. We call this the heliocentric model.

This was a very controversial finding. The Roman Catholic Church, which thought Earth was at the center of the universe, forced Galileo to deny the theory. A man named Giordano Bruno was even burned at the stake for saying he believed in the heliocentric model. After Galileo's death, however, scientists eventually accepted his theory as the truth.

Another important discovery from this era came in 1687 when Sir Isaac Newton announced his theory of gravity. All objects, he said, have gravity, which means they attract other objects; the more massive the object, the stronger the pull. So the sun, as the most massive object in the solar system, has the most powerful gravity. It holds the solar system together, keeping the planets in their revolutions—and keeping them from hurtling into space!

Nicolaus Copernicus (left) showed that the sun is the center of our solar system. Sir Isaac Newton (right) proved that the sun's gravity keeps the planets from drifting into space.

INTO THE SPACE AGE

The telescope taught scientists a great deal about the sun—but not everything. As recently as two hundred years ago, a British astronomer named William Herschel believed the sun was a planet, like Earth, and that creatures "adapted to the peculiar circumstances of that vast globe" lived there.

In the twentieth century, however, new technology has given us a much more accurate picture of the sun.

To look at the sun safely—without blinding themselves—astronomers now use solar telescopes. These special telescopes have mirrors that reflect an image of the sun onto a viewing table. They are usually located on high mountaintops because clean, cloudless skies are needed to properly observe the sun.

One of the most powerful tools used to study the sun is called a *spectroscope*. Every beam of light from the sun carries information about the place it came from—like a fingerprint or a secret code. A spectroscope can crack this code by breaking the beam of light into hundreds of dark, narrow lines. By studying these

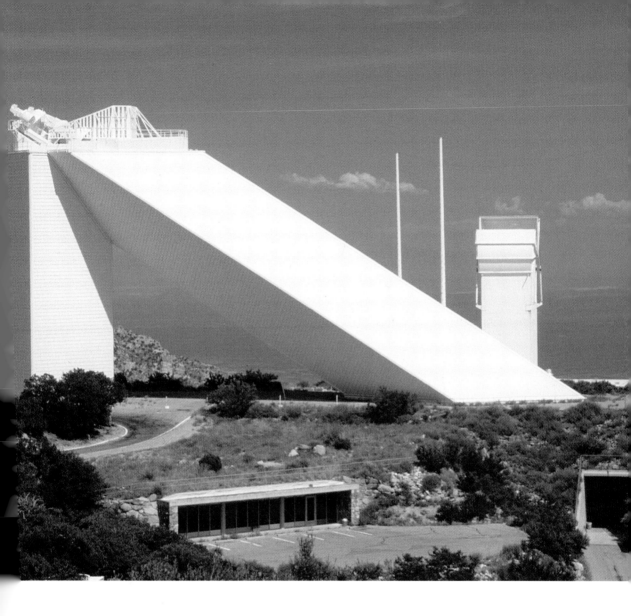

This telescope at the National Solar Observatory uses a 60-inch mirror to reflect the sun's image — otherwise astronomers studying the sun would damage their eyes.

Scientists test the *Helios 2* space probe to make sure it can withstand the sun's intense rays. *Helios 2* traveled to within 28 million miles (45 million km) of the sun.

lines, astronomers can learn a great deal about what makes up the sun.

In 1976, an unmanned *probe* named *Helios 2* got closer to the sun than any human ever could. With its sensitive instruments protected from the intense heat, it got within 28 million miles (45 million km) of the sun's surface and relayed much important data back to scientists on Earth.

The year 1990 brought a new solar detective into play: another robotic probe named *Ulysses*. An 816-pound (370-kg) craft, it was launched by the space shuttle *Discovery* to go where no probe has gone before: the north and south poles of the sun.

By the end of its 2-billion-mile (3.2-billion-km) journey, *Ulysses* will give scientists enough new information to rewrite all the textbooks about the sun.

A STAR IS BORN

CHAPTER THREE

In the beginning there was . . . *nothing.*

Well, not exactly nothing. But billions of years ago there was no sun, no Earth, no solar system. Instead, there existed a huge cloud of dust and gas—mostly hydrogen—that swirled and drifted its way through the galaxy. (Today, astronomers using powerful telescopes can see similar clouds floating in distant space.)

Then, about five billion years ago, there were enough *atoms* (or basic building blocks) of hydrogen in the cloud for gravity to begin pulling them together. As they were pulled together, the cloud started to shrink. And as the cloud grew smaller, it became denser. Soon the atoms were moving so fast that the cloud began to glow.

When the cloud got hot enough, the electrons and protons in the hydrogen atoms flew apart. Sometimes two protons would collide and fuse, or stick together. This continued until atoms of helium were formed.

Scientists call this process *fusion*, because particles are literally fusing together to form new atoms. When fusion happens, energy is also produced—tremendous amounts of energy, in the form of light and heat.

This energy made the cloud start to expand. At the same time, however, gravity was still trying to pull the atoms closer together. Pushing and pulling, like a tug-of-war, these two forces balanced each other. And so the cloud settled into a glowing ball—our sun.

With a sun now at the middle, our solar system began to take shape. The leftover gas and dust settled into a cloud circling this young star. Over many millions of years this cloud formed into nine planets (including Earth) and an assortment of moons, asteroids, comets, and meteoroids.

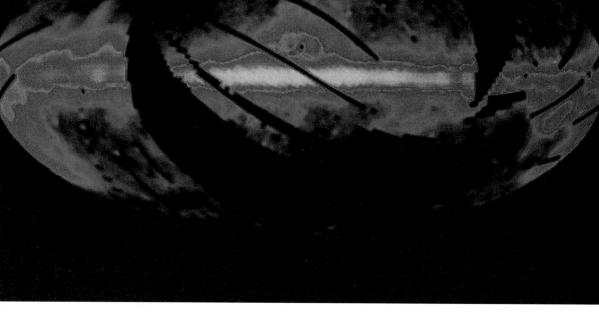

NASA's Cosmic Background Explorer was designed to study background radiation in the solar system. In this image, the intense yellow color at the center shows the highest concentration of dust particles in the Milky Way.

THE FUSION FURNACE

Five billion years later, the sun continues to glow, thanks to the power of fusion. Hydrogen is fused into helium; energy is released in the form of gamma rays, a type of radiation that is invisible and very, very hot. This process is carried out tens of trillions of times every second.

You could think of the sun as a giant furnace. But the sun is much more efficient than a furnace at turning fuel into energy. A lump of coal the size of the sun would burn itself out in about three thousand years (and give off much less heat). As it loses hydrogen and gains helium, the sun will also burn itself out. But it will be a very long time—five billion years—before the sun runs out of hydrogen fuel.

A better way to think of the sun is to compare it with a hydrogen bomb. The hydrogen bomb (or H-bomb) also uses fusion to create enormous amounts of energy, which it releases as gamma rays. The deadliest weapon ever invented, it can level everything in its path for miles and miles. Although a hydrogen bomb blast lasts just a short while, the sun is a continuous hydrogen bomb that will give us energy for billions of years.

Thanks to fusion, the sun is the only object in our solar system that gives off light and heat of its own. The planets and moons merely reflect the sun's powerful light.

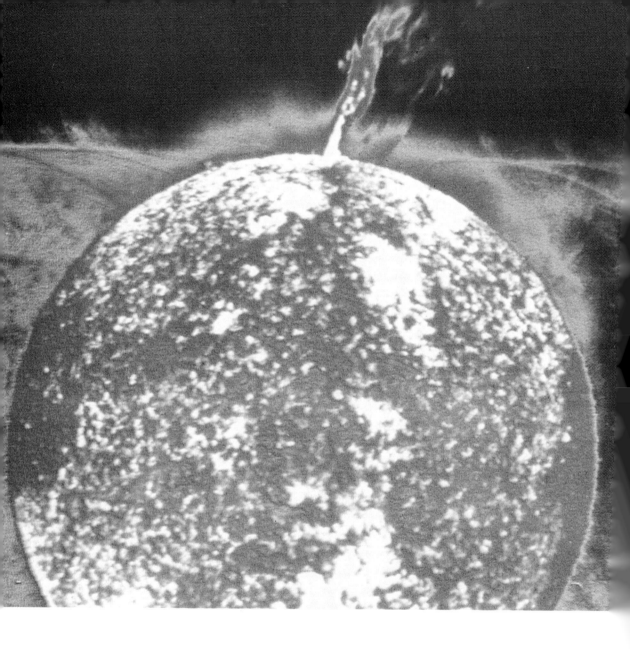

This fiery orb is the only object in our solar
system that actually creates its own light and
heat, thanks to a process called fusion.

INSIDE THE SUN

Where does fusion take place? In the *core*, or center, of the sun.

Though they can't get anywhere near the sun's core, scientists think it's about the size of Jupiter, the biggest planet in the solar system. It is very hot, reaching temperatures of 27 million° F (15 million° C). And it is very *dense*. Gas at the sun's surface is much thinner than the air we breathe on Earth. But if you burrow deeper inside, the gas gets thicker; it is squashed by the sun's strong gravitational pull. Gas at the core is about one hundred times denser than most metals—in fact, a box of gas from the sun's core would be twelve times heavier than a box of the same size filled with lead.

Because the core is so dense, it's a tough place to escape. When gamma rays released by fusion try to leave, they keep colliding with the tightly packed atoms. As a result, it takes the gamma rays nearly thirty thousand years to reach the sun's surface! By contrast, it takes them less than nine minutes to travel the 93 million miles (149 million km) to Earth.

In other words, the light hitting Earth today was actually created back when saber-toothed tigers prowled our planet!

THE RAGING SUN

CHAPTER FOUR

Here on Earth, the sun seems like a constant, friendly presence, providing us with heat and light, driving our winds and weather, and growing our green plants.

Up close and personal, however, the sun is anything but friendly. Its outer layers are a raging inferno—searingly hot, bubbling, and bursting with gigantic explosions. In 1801, a British astronomer believed the sun might be inhabited, but we know today that its fiery surface is hardly fit for man, woman, or beast!

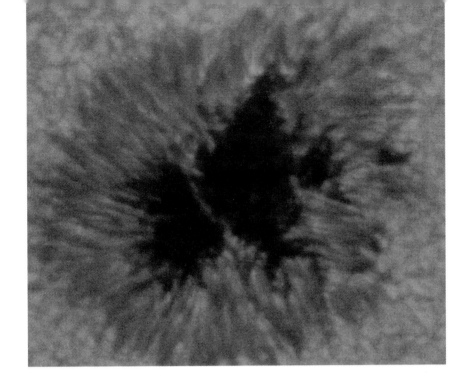

Seen up close, the photosphere begins to show distinct features — a sunspot (center) surrounded by granules, which are evidence of superheated convective cells down below.

THE PHOTOSPHERE

To the naked eye (again, NEVER gaze directly at the sun) the *photosphere* looks like the sun's surface—although, as we learned earlier, a ball of gases like the sun doesn't have a true "surface."

The photosphere (meaning "sphere of light") is an area of great movement and turmoil. Hot gases from deep inside the sun rise up, cool off, and then sink back down again. These superheated clouds of gas are called *convective cells*. As they reach the surface, they look like freckles—these are called *granules*. One scientist compared the appearance of granules to a pot of boiling rice.

The temperature of the photosphere is about 10,000° F (5,500° C), much cooler than what lies below and above. Yet it's the photosphere that sends heat and light into space. These waves travel through space at 186,300 miles (298,080 km) per second, reaching Earth in a little more than eight minutes.

THE CHROMOSPHERE

Traveling away from the sun, the *chromosphere* is the next layer we encounter.

Normally we cannot see the chromosphere, because it's hidden in the bright glare of the photosphere. The best time to see it is during a total eclipse, when the moon passes between us and the sun and blots out the sun's disk. The chromosphere then appears (for a brief time) as a thin pink ring around the edge of the sun.

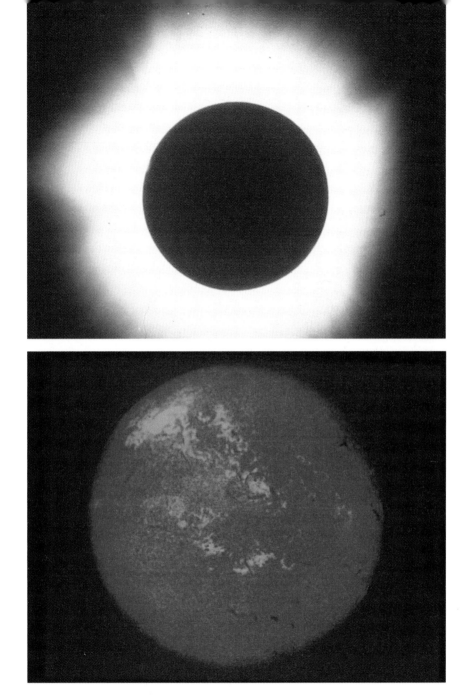

The chromosphere is best seen during a total solar eclipse (above). The sun may seem to have a solid surface (below), but it's actually made up entirely of gas.

Hence the name, which means "sphere of color."

The bottom part of the sun's atmosphere, the chromosphere is irregular in shape. Though it averages a few thousand miles deep, its depth can vary from 1,000 to 10,000 miles (1,600 to 16,000 km).

Making the chromosphere very irregular are giant tongues of flame called spicules. These are jets of hot gas that shoot from the chromosphere into the less dense area above. Traveling at speeds of about 17 miles (27 km) per second, they can extend as far as 10,000 miles (16,000 km). To one scientist, spicules make the chromosphere look like a "flaming forest."

THE CORONA

Like the chromosphere, the *corona* is something of a mystery because the brightness of the inner sun makes it hard to see. It is best studied during a total eclipse, when it appears as a pearly white layer that extends out several times the diameter of the sun.

The corona is the top layer of the sun's atmosphere—and a big layer it is! Made up of very hot, very thin gases, it stretches more

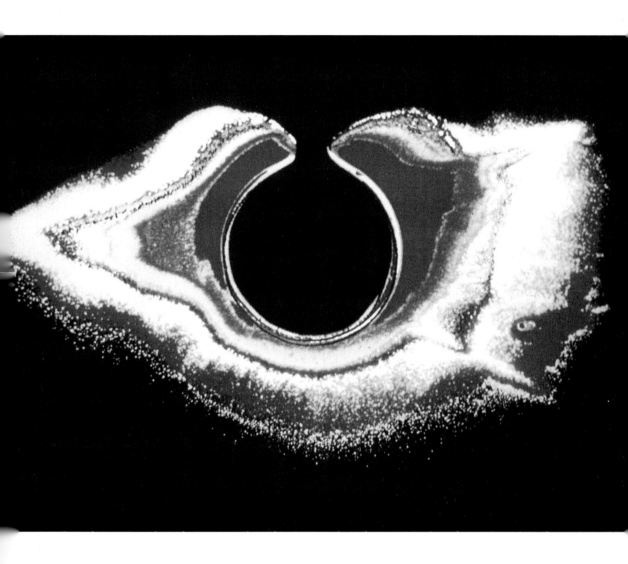

The sun's outer layer, called the corona, stretches
more than 1 million miles (1.6 million km). Its shape
is very irregular, as you can see in this NASA photo.

than 1 million miles (1.6 million km) from the photosphere. It is up to 1 million° F (555,538° C) hotter than the sun's surface, possibly because its gases are being violently vibrated by all the explosions down below.

Because of these high temperatures, the corona is always expanding and changing its shape. Sometimes it travels as far as Jupiter, in gusts known as the *solar wind* (discussed at the end of the chapter).

SUNSPOTS

One of the most interesting—and most puzzling—examples of the incredible turmoil at the sun's surface is the *sunspot*.

As early as 28 B.C., Chinese scientists noticed dark spots on the sun's surface. They thought these blotches were shadows cast by flying birds. In 1610, Galileo used his new telescope to watch these sunspots drift across the surface. His findings angered the Roman Catholic Church, which believed that God's creations had no "imperfections."

Today we know that sunspots are not imperfections, but everyday solar events. They

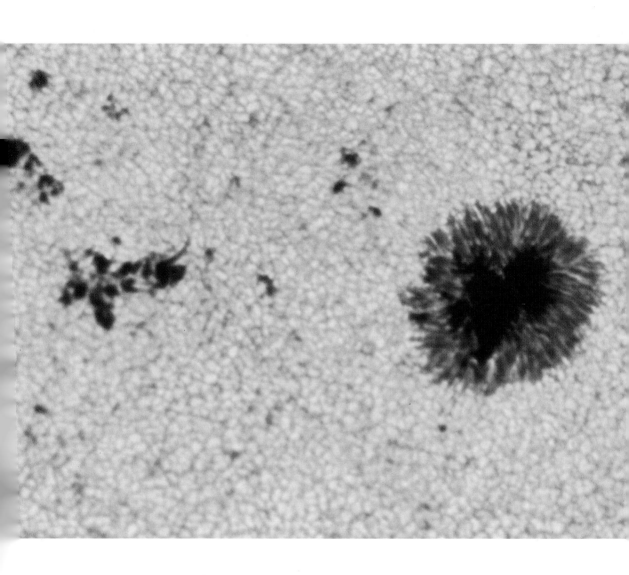

These sunspots are about half as bright as the
nearby surface. They appear dark because
they are cooler than the surrounding gases.

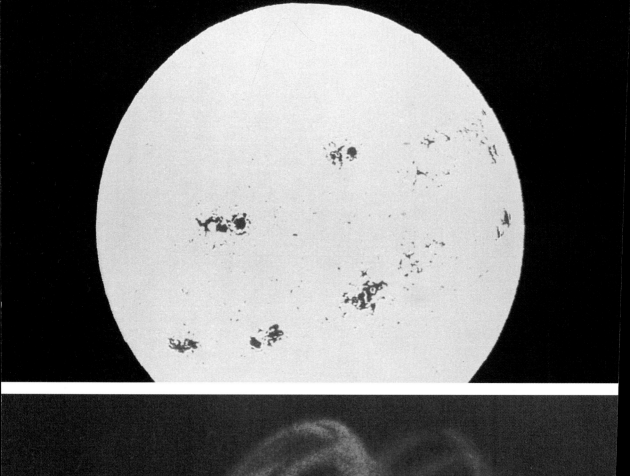

The top picture, called a magnetogram, shows the presence of intense magnetic forces on the sun. These forces run in long strands (below), which burst through the surface and loop back.

appear dark because they're cooler than the surrounding gases, though they're still very hot—about 7,000° F (4,000° C). They range from 500 miles (800 km) in diameter to more than 50,000 miles (80,000 km)—big enough to swallow several Earths.

Sunspots can appear alone, or in groups of more than one hundred. An average sunspot lives for about a week, though they can last for only a few hours or as long as eighteen months.

Beyond these basic facts, scientists don't fully understand sunspots, where they come from, or why they exist. They do know that, like Earth, the sun has a strong magnetic field. Sunspots appear when these magnetic forces break through the sun's photosphere. The magnetic forces slow down the vibration of gas atoms on the surface. These areas will then be cooler and will appear darker than the surrounding area.

Sunspots usually come in pairs because (according to this theory) the magnetic fields run in long strands, like ropes. The ropes burst through the surface and then loop back, forming a second sunspot. The magnetic-field strands of the sun are like the ones running from pole to pole of a bar magnet. Scientists have discovered that the sunspots in each pair have opposite magnetic polarity.

The effect of sunspots on Earth is not known. Scientists are trying to see if there is any connection between sunspots and plant growth or changes in the weather. Maybe we will finally be able to find out how these mysterious spots affect life on our planet Earth.

In 1843, an amateur astronomer named Samuel Heinrich Schwabe noticed that sunspots appear in a sort of cycle. When there are only a few sunspots, it's called a solar minimum; when there are many, it's a solar maximum. The periods between maximums average eleven years, but can vary from seven to as long as seventeen years.

PROMINENCES

Sometimes a sunspot's magnetic forces erupt into space, carrying hot gases with them. These giant flaming arches, called *prominences*, extend into the corona and then loop back. Most are about 100,000 miles (160,000 km) long and 3,000 miles (4,800 km) thick, though they sometimes soar as high as 2 mil-

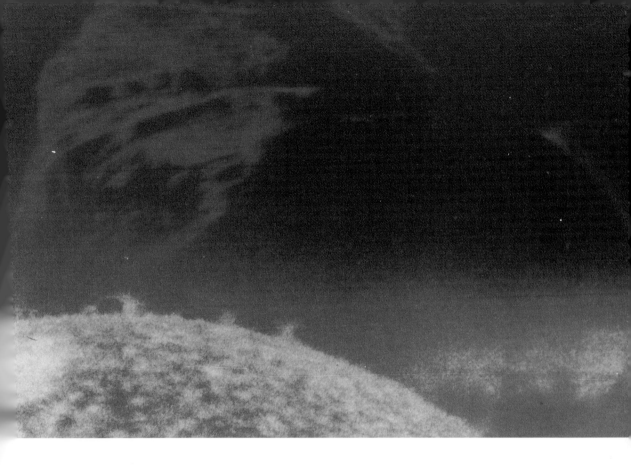

A huge solar explosion sends a flaming arch, called a prominence, into space. Some prominences soar as high as 2 million miles.

lion miles (3.2 million km) above the surface. They usually travel at about 100 miles (160 km) per second, though some move as fast as 830 miles (1,330 km) per second.

Like the corona, prominences are best seen during a total eclipse.

SOLAR FLARES

We've saved the best for last. *Solar flares* are the most spectacular of all the sun's displays, putting the greatest fireworks show on Earth to shame.

Flares are explosions, caused (like sunspots and prominences) by magnetic forces on the sun's surface. Though a flare may last only a few minutes, one such outburst can be as powerful as ten million hydrogen bombs. In fact, a big flare produces enough energy to supply a major city with electricity for 200 million years!

A flare belches billions of tons of solar matter into space—not to mention waves of intense light, heat, and radiation. As we'll learn in the next chapter, this radiation is so powerful it can effect life on Earth.

Particles of matter from flares are carried by the solar wind. The solar wind blows especially hard after a flare, but it is always moving—every second it carries 1 million tons (907,185 metric tons) of the sun into space, at a speed of 200 to 500 miles (320 to 800 km) per second.

Like wind on Earth, the solar wind cannot be seen, but it can be felt. The National

Solar flares, the most spectacular of the sun's eruptions, shoot tongues of flame into space. A big flare like this creates enough energy to power a major city for millions of years.

Aeronautics and Space Administration (NASA) has designed a solar sail that, with the help of solar wind, could push a spacecraft between planets—*without* an engine.

THE SUN ON EARTH

CHAPTER FIVE

What has the sun done for you lately? Well, if you step outside you can see and feel the sun's two most important gifts to Earth: light and heat. Amazingly, that light takes just 8.33 minutes to travel the 93 million miles (150 million km) between the sun and Earth. By contrast, a jet plane traveling 600 miles per hour (965 kmph)—the speed of sound—would take nearly eighteen years to make the same trip.

It's not an exaggeration to say that sunlight is directly responsible for all earthly life; our Earth would be nothing but a boring hunk of rock without it. But when the sun gets agitated, it can drop its friendly face and cause real trouble here on the green planet. All life on Earth depends on the sun's steady output of energy over the years. If the sun brightened or dimmed a great deal, no creatures on Earth could stand the changes.

SOLAR ENERGY

How powerful is the sun's energy? Well, our planet (a small target within the total universe) intercepts only 2.2 billionths of the total energy generated by the sun. Yet this tiny fraction is enough to support all life on Earth!

And this fraction is responsible for every bit of energy here. Even windmills and hydropower plants get their energy from the sun—windmills because the sun causes winds to blow, and hydropower because it causes rivers to flow.

Most of our electricity is generated by burning *fossil fuels*: coal, oil, and natural gas. These too come from sunlight. Before the age of the dinosaurs, plants and tiny sea animals—which relied on the sun to grow—died and were buried. Over millions of years they were com-

In Minnesota, these solar collectors help to heat and cool a large office building. Scientists hope to lessen our use of fossil fuels by harnessing the sun's energy.

pacted underground, until they turned into the fuels we use today. So when we burn coal or oil we're simply letting loose the energy of sunlight that was trapped millions of years ago.

Unfortunately, we are using fossil fuels faster that they can be replaced. Maybe we can find a solution to our energy crisis in the sun—

either by using the sun directly, or learning to imitate it.

Directly, the sun can supply much of our heat and electricity. Solar energy doesn't pollute, it's almost free, and it will never run out (at least not for five billion years or so). In just two weeks, we intercept more energy from the sun than is stored in all the fossil fuels found on Earth— yet most of it is wasted.

Scientists are working on ways to store the sun's power, using solar collectors and solar cells. Someday in the future, we might use giant mirrors to focus the sun's rays on photocells and generate electricity.

Another way to create energy is to mimic the sun's power. Scientists are learning to generate power through hydrogen fusion—the same method used by the sun's core. In this way, maybe we could create a miniature sun here on Earth.

LIFE IN THE FOOD CHAIN

Our bodies also need energy, to run and jump and do homework—and this too comes from the sun.

The sun triggers a process called *photosynthesis* in green plants. Plants trap the sun's energy and turn it into carbohydrates, the basic building blocks for life. When animals eat those plants, the energy is converted by organs in their bodies into an energy form they can use. And when animals eat *those* animals, the carbohydrates are passed up the food chain. So when you eat meat or potatoes, you're actually eating the sun's energy.

WEATHER

What else can the sun do for us? How about controlling our weather?

It's a simple process. The sun's rays (in the form of radiation) hit the ground, and the warm ground heats the air above. Warm air at the equator moves north and south to the cooler regions at the poles, making winds.

The sun also warms the oceans, turning some of the water into vapor. The vapor rises, cools, and forms clouds. When the drops in the clouds get big enough, they fall as rain, sleet, snow, or hail.

SUNSPOTS AND THE "LITTLE ICE AGE"

If the sun drives our weather, could turmoil on the sun (discussed in the last chapter) cause turmoil in Earth's weather?

There are scientists who believe that sunspots do affect our weather. Though they can't explain why, there is proof to back up their theory. Between the years 1645 and 1715, sunspots practically disappeared from the sun's surface. (This seventy-year period is called the Maunder minimum, after the astronomer who first noticed it.) At the same time, Earth was going through a "Little Ice Age," a period of record low temperatures. Glaciers moved farther south than they had been in thousands of years, and Mexican conquistadors marched horses across a frozen Rio Grande.

Was the Little Ice Age the result of the sunspot cycle, or just a coincidence?

Scientists have discovered other periods where low or high sunspot activity corresponded with unusually cold or hot weather here on Earth. They are busy trying to explain this curious discovery.

There are some who think the sunspot cycle affects all sorts of events on Earth—from the rise and fall of the stock market to the length of women's dresses. Most of these people are dismissed as crackpots. But who knows what scientists will learn about sunspots in the future?

THE SOLAR JUNKYARD

Solar activity definitely affects other aspects of life on Earth. Remember solar flares? They belch forth billions of tons of atomic particles into space, which reach Earth in two days.

The Earth is surrounded by a magnetic field "umbrella" that deflects most of the incoming electrons. But some of them get trapped inside this magnetic field, and circle the globe. When they reach the North and South poles, where the magnetic field is weakest, the electrons sink into Earth's atmosphere and collide with nitrogen or oxygen atoms. The electrical current that is generated creates a curtain of red and green light called an *aurora*: either an aurora borealis ("northern lights") or aurora australis ("southern lights"), depending on which pole. This beautiful sight is normally

When electrons from the sun hit Earth's atmosphere,
they create a colorful display called an aurora.
This photo of the northern lights was taken from the
space shuttle *Discovery*.

seen near the poles, though when it is strong it can be viewed as far south as Texas and Florida.

An especially powerful flare bombards Earth with a very large number of particles. These solar storms (also called solar disturbances) can wreak havoc on our planet, knocking out electric power stations, interrupting radio signals, and causing compasses to spin wildly.

During a 1972 flare, a 230,000-volt transformer in British Columbia exploded. During a 1989 flare—one of the biggest in recent history—parts of Montreal were blacked out for nine hours. People even reported that their automatic garage doors were opening and closing on their own! Such is the power of the sun on Earth.

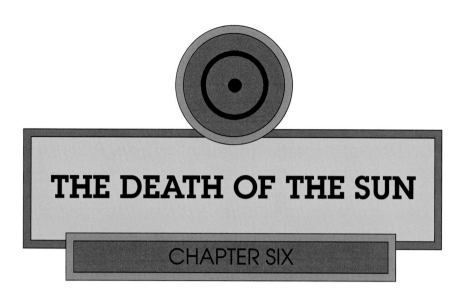

THE DEATH OF THE SUN

CHAPTER SIX

Have you heard the expression, "As sure as the sun will rise in the morning"? Well, someday it won't. Someday the sun won't be there to warm us, grow our plants, give us light.

Don't panic, though. That someday is a long, long time in the future.

As we've learned, the sun exists because of fusion. Every second it turns 600 million tons (544 million metric tons) of hydrogen into helium (and energy). Scientists estimate that the sun has enough fuel to last another five billion years or so.

After that? Well, without the force of fusion pushing out, the sun won't be able to resist its own gravity pulling in, and will start to collapse. The atoms will fall toward each other faster and faster, heating up just like when the sun was born. Only this time, because the hydrogen has been spent, it's helium fusion that will result. Helium fusion releases even more energy than hydrogen fusion, so the sun will become very, very hot and start to expand.

At this point, our sun won't be a yellow dwarf anymore—it will be called a red giant. It will burn maybe one thousand times more brightly than it does now. The outer layers will swell hundreds of times bigger, swallowing up Mercury and Venus—maybe even Earth. Our oceans will boil, and life here will no longer be possible.

The red giant will use up all its helium fuel in a million years or so. The outer layers will expand away into space (the solar wind will be more like a solar hurricane), leaving behind the bare core, a lump about the size of Earth. This star—now called a white dwarf—will burn blue-hot at maybe 216,032° F (120,000° C). It will be very dense; the atoms will be packed so tightly that one cubic inch will weigh more than a ton. And it will be very bright—but because it's so small, it will look faint from Earth. (If there still is an Earth.)

For the next several billion years, the white dwarf will slowly burn out. Eventually it will cool off and become a black dwarf—nothing but a cinder. And that will be the end of our sun.

But don't despair; this won't happen for another five billion years. And who knows what discoveries astronomers will make by then?

Before our sun cools off, maybe we humans will find a new star that can warm, feed, and protect us for another few billion years!

FACT SHEET ON THE SUN

Symbol for the Sun — ⊙

Position — the sun is at the center of our solar system. Its nearest planetary neighbor is Mercury.

Rotation period — the sun's outer layer rotates more rapidly at the equator than at the poles. At the equator, it takes as few as twenty-five Earth days to spin around its axis; at the poles, more than thirty Earth days.

Temperature — ranges from about 10,000° F (6,000° C) at the surface to 27,000,000° F (15,000,000° C) at the center.

Composition — the sun is made up of hot gases, mostly hydrogen (from 75 percent to 90 percent) and helium (from 10 percent to 25 percent). Carbon, nitrogen, and oxygen total less than 1 percent.

Diameter — 865,000 miles (1,393,000 km), wider than one hundred Earths.

Weight — about 2 thousand trillion trillion tons.

Distance from the Earth (depending on orbit) — least: 91,423,000 miles (147,150,000 km); greatest: 94,530,800 miles (152,140,000 km).

GLOSSARY

Astronomer—a scientist who studies the universe beyond Earth

Atmosphere—the gases that surround a star or planet

Atoms—the basic building blocks that make up all matter

Aurora—glowing bands of colored light caused by particles in the solar wind as they strike Earth's atmosphere

Axis—the imaginary line through a heavenly body's center, around which it rotates

Chromosphere—the bottom layer of the sun's atmosphere, lying between the photosphere and the corona

Convective cell—a cloud of superheated gas that rises from deep inside the sun

Core—the innermost part of a star or planet

Corona—the top layer of the sun's atmosphere, a strip of hot, thin gases about a million miles wide

Density—the amount of matter packed into the volume of an object

Fossil fuel—fuels such as coal, oil, and natural gas, which are made from long-dead plants and animals

Fusion—the process that turns hydrogen into helium and creates the sun's energy

Granule—a region on the sun's surface, caused by hot gases rising from deep inside the sun

Gravity—the force that pulls objects toward the center of a planet or star

Magnetic field—the area around a planet or sun in which a magnetic (or attractive) force can be felt

Mass—the amount of matter in an object

Orbit—the curved path of an object moving around another object

Photosphere—the bright visible surface of the sun seen on any clear day

Photosynthesis—the process used by green plants to make their own food using water, air, and the energy from the sun

Probe—an unmanned spacecraft sent to study a planet or heavenly body

Prominence—a fiery cloud of gas, shaped like an arc, that rises high above the sun's surface

Red giant—a star that has used up all of its hydrogen fuel and grown very large; it is much cooler than the sun and emits a reddish light

Solar flare—a sudden burst of light and energy at the sun's surface that sends solar particles into space

Solar system—our sun and all the objects that revolve around it, including the nine planets, their moons, comets, meteors, and asteroids

Solar wind—a stream of tiny particles, including electrons, that escape from the sun and are spewed into space

Spectroscope—an instrument used to study beams of sunlight and learn about the sun's temperature, composition, and magnetism

Spicule—a high-speed jet of gas that shoots up from the chromosphere into the corona

Star—a ball of gases that creates (through fusion) its own heat and light

Sunspot—a cooler, darker area in the photosphere that appears as a dark blemish on the sun's brilliant surface

Total eclipse—a complete darkening of the sun's disk that occurs when the moon passes between Earth and the sun

White dwarf—a small, hot star that has used up all of its helium fuel and stopped making energy

Yellow dwarf—a star that is average in size, brightness, and temperature—like our sun

FOR FURTHER READING

Arnold, Caroline. *Sun Fun*. New York: Franklin Watts, 1981.

Darling, David J. *The Sun: Our Neighborhood Star*. Minneapolis: Dillon Press, 1984.

Lampton, Christopher. *The Sun*. New York: Franklin Watts, 1982.

Petty, Kate. *The Sun*. New York: Franklin Watts, 1985.

Simon, Seymour. *The Sun*. New York: Mulberry Books, 1986.

INDEX

ABOUT THE AUTHOR

Robert Daily received a B.A. in English literature from Carleton College and a master's
degree in English literature from the University
of Chicago. He is a magazine writer for both
adults and children and is also the author of
Mercury, *Earth*, and *Pluto* in the First Book
series. He lives with his wife, Janet, in Chicago.